Captain Moroni

T0272328

written by Tiffany Thomas
illustrated by Nikki Casassa

CFI · An imprint of Cedar Fort, Inc. · Springville, Utah

HARD WORDS:
Moroni, captain, title, liberty

PARENT TIP: If the child struggles with blending consonants, try saying other words with those same blends. Example: brings, bread, brake, brown.

This is Moroni.
He is a man of God.

Moroni is a captain in the Nephite army.

3

The Lamanites are bad.

The Lamanites want to hurt the Nephites.

Captain Moroni
helps the Nephites
fight the Lamanites.

Some Nephites do not want to fight.

Captain Moroni
makes a flag called
the title of liberty.

8

Many Nephites read the
flag and come to help.

The Nephites fight the Lamanites.

The Nephites win.

Captain Moroni is happy.

The end.

ISBN 13: 978-1-4621-4337-5

Published by CFI, an imprint of Cedar Fort, Inc. • 2373 W. 700 S., Suite 100, Springville, UT 84663
Distributed by Cedar Fort, Inc., www.cedarfort.com

Cover design and interior layout design by Shawnda T. Craig
Cover design © 2022 Cedar Fort, Inc.
Printed in China • Printed on acid-free paper
10 9 8 7 6 5 4 3 2 1